AUTHOR/DESIGNER TIMIA J. WILLIAMS
Presents

So, You Need A Designer?

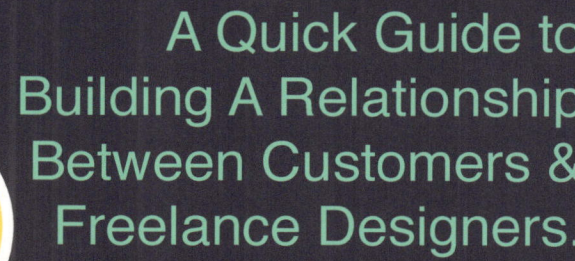

A Quick Guide to Building A Relationship Between Customers & Freelance Designers.

1st Edition

TIMIA J. WILLIAMS

I wanted to inspire new and experienced freelance designers like myself. I know how rough it can be when trying to communicate and work with clients. For the clients it is a fish bowl full of designers. Find a goldfish (I mean designer) that fits you and your needs. This book is for all of you!

Author & Designer: Timia J. Williams
WWW.TIMIAWILLIAMS.COM
Copyright © 2015 Timia J Williams
All rights reserved.
ISBN: 1508557756
ISBN-13: 978-1508557753
Stock images were obtained from www.pixababy.com

CONTENTS

FOR DESIGNERS

Now-a-days things are in digital so if you just have a traditional portfolio this will not matter to you. If you do have a digital portfolio pay attention these are some things that definitely need to be apart of your online portfolio:

About: Have an about me section. You want your clients to have some information about your education or experience. Also, refer to yourself in third person.

Resume: Have a way that your client can review or download your resume (PDF recommended). Your Resume must be clear and honest. You do not want false information that will bite you in the butt later (Design Karma)!

Images: Put your best 6-10 images on your portfolio site. You don't want to give too much away. Just give enough so your client can see your style and skill.

Logo and Menu: Make sure your logo (if you have one) is easy to spot and your menu bar is easy to navigate. You want your client to find everything on your site easily. (This is especially important for Web Designers)

Contact: Your contact information is one, if not, the most important thing to have visible on your portfolio. You want your client to be able to call you, email you, or find you, if necessary, on social media (i.e. Facebook, LinkedIn, and etc).

Tips

✓ If you do not have an online portfolio or you aren't capable of designing one from scratch you can always use sites like Wix, Wordpress, Behance, Tumblr, and other already built template sites. They are just as effective as a from scratch site. (Sorry web designers!)

✓ Always be honest about your work. Don't show the client work of someone else.

✓ Never advertise above your expertise. If your skills do not comply to the clients expectations simply explain this to them. You don't want to take on more than you can manage.

✓ Make some promotional items to promote yourself on and off the internet: Business cards, flyer's, ads, etc.

✍️ CONTRACTS/PROPOSALS

You are going to come across clients who will try and get over on you. Sometimes you will find a client who wants to do business but they are trying to get something for nothing. You don't want that. You can eliminate these clients immediately by motioning that they sign a contract or proposal. Having documentation before starting any job gives you a bit of insurance that your client is serious about their business. Below are some key things that should be in and explained in your contract or proposal:

Logo: Once again it is important to have your brand on all of your documentations.

Your Contact Information: Of course you want to put your information on the document in case the client have any concerns and questions

Clients Contact Information: have the clients phone number and email address in order to keep in contact in case of changes.

Payment Structure: You want to keep a payment schedule or structure to keep track of due payments and fees.

Terms and Agreements: Cliche to say but make sure you cross your t's and dot your i's! Be sure that your words are put into the correct context and everything is signed and dated by you and your client.

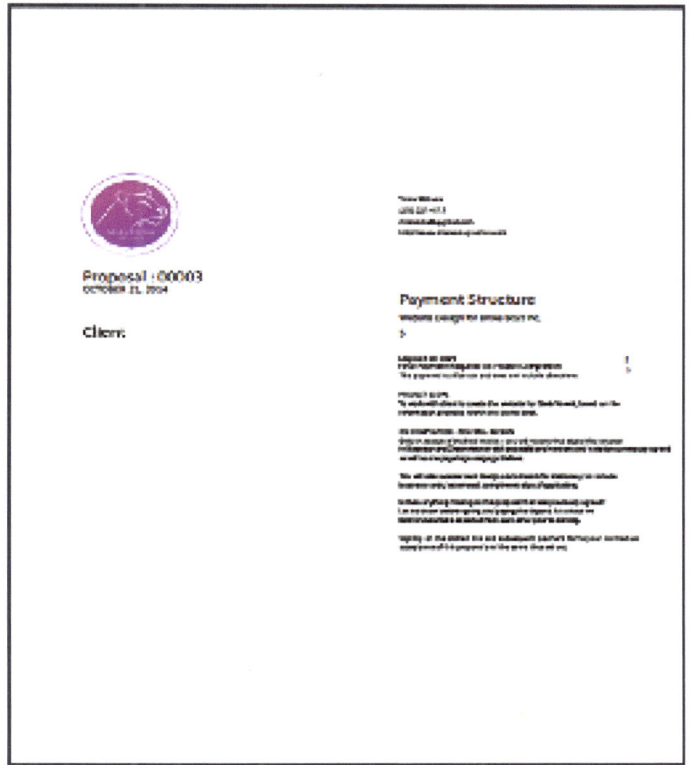

Tips

 Have someone like a lawyer look over your document to make sure you word and elaborate the terms and conditions clearly.

 Make copies of every agreement and changes made to the document.

 Have serial numbers to keep track of your clients. You want to keep your documents organized

 Keep the clients contact information up to date. It is not professional to have outdated information especially if there are issues with the clients agreement.

📰 PAYMENT PLANS

Money. Money. Money. Money. This is where it can get a bit awkward and uncomfortable. But hey you want to get paid for your craft right? After creating, signing, and agreeing with your contract/proposal, it is time to get down to business. Here are some things that need to be discussed and acknowledged when making monetary exchanges with your clients.

Payment Plans: It is a good idea to make schedule plans for payments that are due. This will help you along with your contract to keep up with payments and overall due dates.

Payment arrangements: Having payment arrangements are important. You want to have a way to get compensated. Maybe meeting at a safe location to exchange cash or having an online platform like PayPal to receive money.

Invoice: It is the same as having a receipt. If you are doing payments with PayPal invoices are available on the profile. If you are receiving payments in person you should get a receipt/invoice book. (Also we're designers, we can always design our own invoices!)

Alterations and Fees: You may decide in your contract to have an hourly or flat rate. Either way, remember to accommodate for any alterations that the client may want done, they will want changes, this way they aren't getting over on their agreement.

Tips

 **GET PAID FIRST!** You should never start a project without receiving partial, half, or full payment. How you schedule your payment is up to you.

 If you are doing payments online get an account like PayPal, which is secure and easy to use. You can order a PayPal Business Debit Card to have access to your payment.

 If you are doing payments in person make sure you have receipts or invoices on hand. Invoices are security for keeping track of payments as well.

 It would be a good idea to get a card reader like Square or a PayPal money reader. They are free and convenient. They are great for those 'I don't have cash on me' clients.

♟ CONCEPTS/CREATIVE FREEDOM

You will have clients who have some ideas of what they may or may not want in their design. Then you have the clients who don't have a clue. Either way you're the Designer. Before starting work it should be asked, for the clients who don't have a clue, if it is okay if you can have creative freedom. Having creative freedom is a good way to show you style and skills to your client and it gives you a chance to be more interactive with them.

Samples: If you decide to send samples to your client, be sure to have a water-mark on the document to prevent plagiarizing. You want to give at least 5 different concepts for the clients who don't have any ideas. Show too many they will get picky (we don't want that!) If you don't show enough it will turn into a long drawn out process that can interfere with your schedule.

Clients with concepts: For the clients with ideas and concepts, you want to give them what they want. Make suggestions, this can help those clients understand the design process and what should and shouldn't be done.

Explain: Help your clients understand why they can not use a certain font, or mascot, or certain images on Google. They do not understand but you do.

Quality: Whatever you do you want to present a quality piece of work you want you're clients to be at awe, when you present them with the final draft of whatever the project may be.

Tips

✓ Get an account with Shutterstock or Getty images. This way you can have access to royalty-free images.

✓ Always check and see whatever, design, fonts, phrases, and etc are not already copy-written. This is your responsibility as a designer.

✓ Remember to water mark whatever work you are sending over.

✓ Try to keep the conceptual/idea process quick. You don't want to spend the first phrase of the project on email tag.

✓ Check for misspelled words, or any flaws in your project. Remember you want to send quality work, mistake free!

⏰ SETTING BOUNDARIES

Sometimes you have to put your foot down with clients. Yes, they are paying you to do their design but you do not work for them. You work for yourself. You need to make it known what you do and do not allow with your business.

Business Hours: You should make it clear what your availability is. You do not want a client calling you in the middle of the night when you are trying to watch your favorite television show. Or trying to get some sleep. Give them business hours that best fit you. You're a freelancer, schedule at your own risk, just remember to consider other clients.

Text Messages: This is not a professional way to contact a business unless you are order pizza from Pizza Hut. No client should be texting you unless you allow them to. If a new client tries to contact you this way, it's an automatic red flag.

Micro-managing: You are the Designer. You're the professional. You don't need anyone breathing down you back about what you already know how to do. Also you don't need anyone pestering you about when things are to be done. That's why you have a schedule.

Adding on Extra: Clients will try to tack on extra to the project. Do not allow this to happen. Establish this in your contract.

Tips

 Having business hours will keep pesky and troublesome clients off of your back.

 A suggestion is to get a separate phone for your business and a separate phone for your personal use. This way you can choose your time of availability without shutting the rest of the world out.

 Set up your voice mail and make sure you announce you business hours during the message.

 Add your availability to you online portfolio.

 Do not allow micro-managing. Be passive-aggressive with clients who do walk that line. Just explain to them that you are perfectly capable of completing the task.

Sometimes you have to put your foot down with clients. Yes, they are paying you to do their design but you do not work for them. You work for yourself. You need to make it known what you do and do not allow with your business.

Keep Calender: Keep organized with a calender of some sort. You want to map out what clients are priorities and what clients don't have to be completed top soon.

File Type: You want to make sure you are using and sending the correct file when working with clients. Your client should never get the final file until they have completed their payments. So be careful when sending out files that are working files. My suggestion is to put the individual files in separate folders.

Files: You also may want to name folders for each of you clients so that you don't accidentally save the wrong design or project to the wrong person. You can keep this is a directory folder named 'Clients'. This will also keep your desktop from getting clutter.

Back up: Always remember to back up everything you do. You should purchase an external drive for more memory and space especially for those who have a large clientèle. Also while working save your progress every chance you get so your work is always updated (and so you wont go crazy in case Illustrator decides to crash!)

Tips

✓ It is always a good idea to constantly back up your work. It is devastating to do all that work and lose it. It's more devastating to tell a client you lost their files.

✓ USB's are good, But Dropbox is better. Get a Dropbox or even Google Drive to keep back up documents on.

✓ When sending clients files make sure you are sending the correct file type. Also if they do not understand the differences, explain the difference it will prevent a disaster. (Trust me!)

✓ Either keep a spreadsheet with all your clients and their project schedules or make folders specifically for them on your desktop to keep organized. And remember....Back it up!!!!

 CUSTOMER SERVICE

To wrap the Designers section up, I want to talk about customer service. It is important to make your client feel special. Even if you have more clients, you do not want to rush any job. You want to give them your best work. Doing this will get you more clients and referrals.

Touch base: During your time working with the client just touch bases every once in a while. Even if your schedule is getting hectic it is always good to inform your client in case you are getting close to a deadline.

Keep in Touch: After you complete a project, keep in touch. It's always good to keep your network in tact. Email your clients every once in a while, just to say hello. It will keep you fresh in their minds. This will also show great customer service.

Leave Behinds: When you complete a project with a client, give them something to remember you by. You will want to give them a business card or maybe a nice key chain. This will also keep you in mind when it comes time to do another project.

Tips

✓ Even if it's just to say hello, email or give you client a call.

✓ Leave behinds are nice when you have a new client that you are working with or just finished a project with. This will help you keep a client and gain more, from you presentation.

✓ We freelancers have a hard time finding work, but if you do a good and quality job, referrals will have you flooded with clients.

✓ Build trust. Having a client is like being in a professional relationship. They have to trust you with everything, their money, their ideas, and so much more. Make them feel comfortable and happy that they've had the pleasure of working with a great designer.

FOR CLIENTS

 COME PREPARED

You have no clue of what you want. You don't know the first thing about design. You just want a logo for your business or a website for your Great Aunts bakery. Well this section of the book is for you my lovely clients!

Ideas: If you do have ideas of what you are trying to achieve, come prepared. Bring some sketches, even if they aren't the best looking, it gives the designer an insight into what is going on in you mind. Bring a color palette (you know the colors that you would like to use) it will help and your designer will love you!

No Ideas: Don't worry about not having ideas. That is why you are searching for a designer in the first place. Just remember to let them be a designer. You can not have an idea and then get picky about what the designer comes up with. (See page 25)

The Dreamer: You the client who has the best idea for, lets say, a ice-cream/taco truck. You got all of the details of what you want it to look like and all but you don't have a designer to bring your dream to life or you have a great designer in mind but you don't have the funds (see page 23 for more details)

Research: You do not want to come to a designer with an idea you saw on Google. If you have seen it on Google then pretty much the whole world has too. Do research on your niche and get ideas but don't try and copy anyone else's.

Tips

✓ If you are an already established business but you are looking to upgrade your brand, let the designer know. You do not want them coming in and changing too much you just want them to tweak it and fluff it up a bit.

✓ If you are using images for certain types of projects such as a website or brochure, bring those images with you. Make sure they are royalty-free images or hire a photographer to take the images you need.

✓ Remember to research your designer before reaching out to them. They may not be capable of your task and you don't want to waste their time or your own.

✓ If you have a million ideas, that's great, but if you find a designer and you aren't prepared to sign a contract or pay, be prepared to get the cold shoulder. Again you don't want to waste anyones time. Time is money!

$ BUDGET/PAYMENT PLAN

Freelance does not mean free. Your designer is expected to get compensated for any kind of time that they put in. You want to make sure there aren't any mix ups and misunderstandings when it comes time to pay.

Payment Plans: As with a designer It is a good idea to make schedule plans for payments that are due.

Budget: So you may want a lot of work done but you can't afford to pay for it all at once. Have a budget. Pay for what you can afford at the time. You can your designer can always make arrangements later on.

Invoice: Keep your receipts and invoices handy! Just in case something comes up that may need changing. Also these can be written off for taxes.

Alterations and Fees: This goes along with budgeting. Unless agreed upon you should take into consideration that you may want to add on or alter something in your design. Budget in alteration fees, designers do charge for any extra work that needs to be done.

Tips

 Make sure upon meeting with your designer and signing your contract, that you have the first down payment on hand. Be sure to ask how the designer takes their payment. Some may only want cash and others may   ask for debit or credit.

 Don't forget to ask for a copy of the proposal and an invoice. This will keep you on board with whats going on with your design and expenses

 Fees should be accounted for when budgeting. You don't want to keep paying a fee every time you make a change.

 Make sure to read the fine print in the contract so that you don't get taken advantage of, it is best to bring a lawyer or someone who can read it over with you.

 HAVE AN OPENED MIND

Some clients do not know what they want. You may! But remember you are not the designer. So if your designer has suggestions about certain concepts or ideas... Be open minded!

Trends in Design: in the industry there are certain requirements when it comes to designing. You should listen to you designer when it come to understanding the trends of the industry. You may want something done one way but that may not work out best for you in the end. Your designer knows whats best for you!

Your Opinion: Of course you will still have your opinions on what they design especially if it something you don't like. State your opinion but do not sabotage the design. Just be honest if you don't like something let them know that you don't like it.

Communication: Ask for updates on the design. Ask the designer for their opinions on certain ideas you may have. Even if it isn't directly a design question it is always a great idea to keep open communication.

Research: Don't forget to do your own research in the mean time. You don't have to go to design school to get insight on what's happening in the industry. It will also impress your designer if you know some of the terms and lingo.

Tips

 Do your own research. Look up some trends and upcoming things in the industry, it will help you understand the point of view of your designer.

 Learn the language of your designer. It makes communication go a lot smoother if you are both on the same page.

 Your opinion still matters. It is your business or concept that you are trying to bring to life. Just understand where you designer is coming from.

 Ask for updates on your design and if you want changes because you are inspired by another design, inform your designer in enough time to make revisions.

⮂ NO FLIP FLOPS

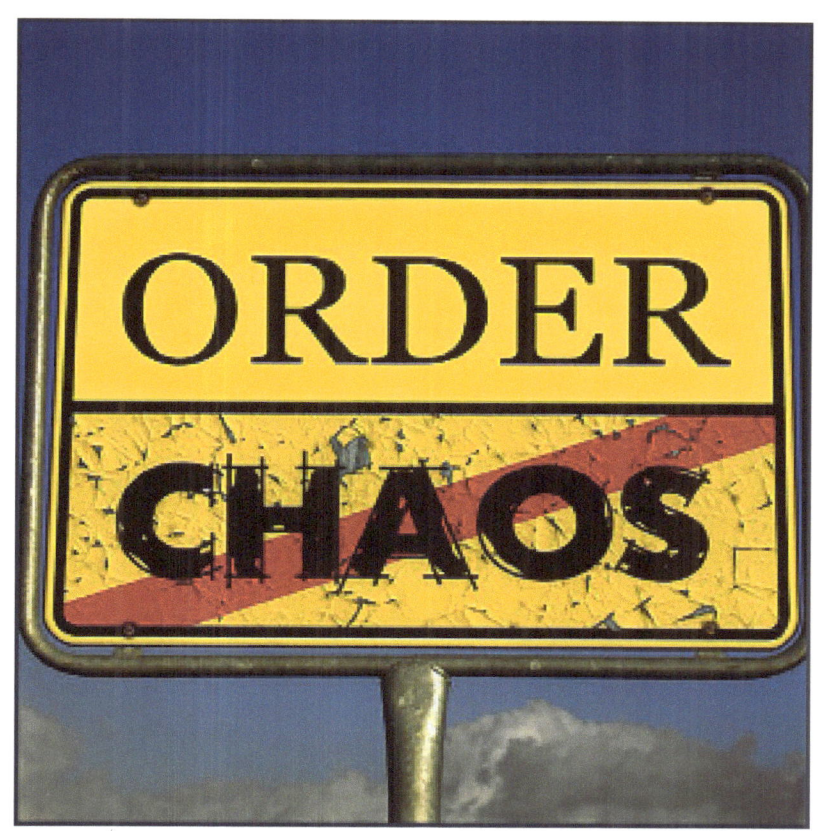

This section is for all you flip flopper's out there! Do not flip flop. What is flip flopping you may ask? It's a term I am using that defines clients who don't really know what they want. Below are some things that may help keep chaos from occurring.

Time is money: You have agreed to have your work completed by a certain date. If you keep changing concepts and ideas, it will eventually cut into the time that is needed to complete your project.

Being mindful: Designers have enough on their plate. Be mindful of the task that you are asking for your designer to do. Your designer may start feel overwhelmed with the pressure of pleasing you.

Changes cost: With all of the changes you want made it will start to add up and if you remember in the budget section you have to keep in mind your fees. Constantly changing your mind about ideas will cost you.

Mistakes: Changing up things can cause a disaster for both parties. Asking for too many changes can become confusing when saving and sending files.

Tips

 If you are a flip flopper be prepared to pay for alterations and fees. Having a designer redesign something over and over can become frustrating and time consuming

 Be prepared as possible. Changing your mind to often can cause confusion. It may lead to mistakes and file mix ups.

 Be honest with your designer about your feelings on the design. Don't nod your head and smile if you aren't completely satisfied but at the same time, don't throw a tantrum.

⚠ RESPECTING BOUNDARIES

As for any business their are policies and regulations that need to be followed. This goes for freelance designers and their clients. Your designer is working for his or her self and do not need a anyone interfering with the way that they running their business.

Business Hours: Please be respectful of your designers time. Do not call after business hours it is inappropriate and inconsiderate. Also remember, you may not be their only client and your project may not be of urgency. If they do not have specific hours, email them if you feel it's too late or early.

Text Messages: Texting is not professional. If you are inquiring to do business with a designer, call them or email them.

Making the Price: You are not the manager of the Designer. What you and your designer may have agreed upon on rates may be different than what the next person may have. Do not quote rates to other potential clients. Ask your designer first is it okay to give the client their number so that they could make their own agreement.

Micro-managing: This will cause a lot of controversy between you and you designer. They are professionals and would like to have the creative freedom allowed to complete the task and satisfy their clients. You're paying them to make your work look good so, sit back and relax!

Tips

✓ Your designer is a freelancer. They do not work for you, so they are not to be on call like a doctor.

✓ Take in to consideration that your designer may have other clients you do not want to interfere with other projects especial if your work isn't due at the current time.

✓ Do not Micro manage! Let the designer do their job. Your job is to critique not take control of the situation.

✓ Keep in contact just do it at the respected hours that the designer require. If the problem is urgent email them and try calling them at the next and earliest business hour.

Now you have others who are impressed with you business cards, signs, website and etc. They ask you who did them and how much did it cost you? Now it's your opportunity to share your resources. This will not only benefit your designer, but it will also benefit you.

Contact Information: Lead the new client to the designers online website. This gives them an idea of what they might be looking for. It will also give them options to find another designer if they do not find the other work that the designer has meet their needs.

Let the designer know: Don't just give someone your clients information. Check with them and let them know that you know people interested in their work and ask them if it is okay to give the client their information.

Remember that business card?: Give them a business card. That's what your designer gave them to you for. Spread the word!

Speak no evil: Speak highly of your designer, give them credit. They put hard work into your design or project, the least you can do is bring them more business. They will most likely reward you with discounts for bringing them more people.

Tips

 Keep all business cards and numbers for your designer at hand. You never know who will need one soon.

 Designers appreciate being referred, but inform them about a referral so that they will be on the look out for new emails and phone calls.

 Speak highly of your designer. Sometimes designer give referral discounts to clients who send them business. This could be good to have in future projects

 Be sure to tell whoever you refer to see the availability of the designer. Give them the appropriate business hours and the best way to get in contact with the designer.

☺RESPECT THE DESIGNER

Your designer is taking a lot of time and creativity to help your vision become reality. You want to show them the respect that they deserve. (Give respect to get respect) Leaving a bad taste in your designers mouth can have horrid consequences in the future for you. Here are some things to keep in mind:

Changes in your design: Your designer has his or hers own style. You do not want to have them work on something and then take it to another designer to get it altered. No two designers are alike and you are opening up Pandora's box.

Disagreements: Every relationship has its ups and downs. So if you are having a "break-up with your designer, don't bad mouth them to other designers and potential clients. It is not professional of you. You wouldn't want your designer to tell other designers you're a bad client would you?

Terms and Agreements: Make sure that you follow your contractual agreement. Breaking contract can lead to some serious legal obligations that no one wants to deal with. Make sure all of your payments are completed before receiving you final draft of you project.

Tips

✓ If you decide you want the color changed or maybe the font removed take it to the original Designer. This person knows the work and it is their style.

✓ Unless you have a background in design and have the proper programs do not try and tweak anything. You could ruin the files if they are overwritten when saved. Don't manipulate the design. This means don't stretch it out and skew it from it's original form.

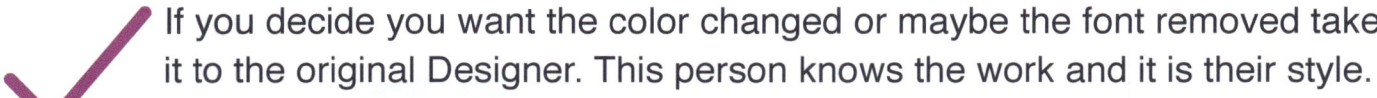

✓ Don't bad talk your designer. If there were some misunderstandings simply state it to the designer in a polite but firm manner. You do not want to play the blame game and point fingers. (Bad business, bad, bad business.)

✓ Do not take any art work from one designer to another one in the middle of a project. You do not want one designing manipulating another's work. (That's like getting Picasso to repaint the Sistine chapel...You get my drift.)

HERE'S A SCENARIO!

🗨 KAREN & LIONEL'S BEST CASE

This scenario is just an example of what a real encounter between a Designer and Client could be like. This is how it should be handled in most cases.

Lionel: "Hello. My name is Lionel, I am in the search for a Graphic Designer that is local. You were recommended by a friend"

Karen: "Hi, Lionel, I am Karen. Thank you for considering me. What can I help you with?"

Lionel: "Well, I am starting a contracting business. I am looking for a logo, a website, and some promotional items to start."

Karen: "Okay, I think I can assist you with your inquiries. What is your availability? I would like to meet with you to discuss and go over my contract, and rates."

Lionel: "We can meet this afternoon. Maybe a coffee shop in the city?"

Karen: "Perfect! I can meet you at 3 o' clock."

Both Karen and Lionel should be on time for the meeting. They both need to set a great first impression and build trust in one another because money is involved in the process.

Lionel: "Is it possible, I would like to take a look at some of your previous clients.

Karen: "Absolutely!. Here you go."

Karen came prepared with her portfolio. She was recommended to by Lionel's friend, so he may or may not have had the opportunity to look at it online. Karen has also bought with her a copy of her resume, the contract, and her card reader. She also has a invoice book to give Lionel his receipt promptly.

Karen: "Do you already have ideas for your logo design?"

Lionel: "None. I was going to leave the design completely up to you"

Karen: "Great! Here's my contract and rates. We can schedule payments but I do require a down payment to begin."

Lionel: "Okay no problem! The only thing is I don't have cash on me just my cards"

Karen: "That's okay, I have my card reader."

Lionel: "So glad that you are organized and prepared. I feel comfortable and look forward to doing business with you. What is your business hours?

Karen: "I am available by phone Monday thru Friday, 9AM-5PM"

Lionel: "Okay! Well it has been a pleasure to meet you Karen. I will be in touch"

KAREN & LIONEL'S WORST CASE

This scenario is just an example of what could go wrong in an encounter between a Designer and Client.

Lionel: "Hello. My name is Lionel, I am in the search for a Graphic Designer that is local. I texted you yesterday did you get it?"

Karen: "I would like to inform you that I do not answer text messages from new clients."

Lionel: "Sorry. I am starting a contracting business. I am looking for a logo, a website, and some promotional items to start."

Karen: "Okay, Right now I my business hours are over for the day. What is your availability? I would like to meet with you to discuss and go over my contract, and rates."

Lionel: "We can meet tomorrow afternoon. Maybe a coffee shop in the city?"

Karen: "Great. I can meet you at 3 o' clock."

Karen is on time for the meeting. But Lionel shows up almost 30 minutes late. He has already made a bad first impression over the phone and now is late for their meeting

Lionel: "My apologies for being late. I got stuck in traffic."

Karen: "Apologies accepted. Now to discuss business. I have an appointment with another client."

Karen: "Do you already have ideas for your logo design?"

Lionel: "None. I was going to leave the design completely up to you"

Karen: "Great! Here's my contract and rates. We can schedule payments but I do require a down payment to begin."

Lionel: "Oh, I don't have cash on me. I wasn't expecting to pay today."

Karen: "Well I do not start work without receiving a down payment to secure the project."

Lionel: "Maybe we can meet another time."

Karen: "I am going to have to decline, sir."

Lionel: "Okay. Sorry to have wasted your time."

Karen came prepared with her portfolio. Karen has also bought with her a copy of her resume, the contract, and her card reader. She also has a invoice book. Lionel was not prepared to do any business. He was late for their appointment and did not have a concept or idea. Karen would not have had an issue with him not having an idea but he did not bring the cash needed in order for her to begin his project.

Useful Links

Here are some useful links for Designers. These are just a few recommended but there are many, many more to choose from on the web!

Online Portfolio Sites

http://www.wix.com

https://www.behance.net

https://www.wordpress.com

https://www.tumblr.com

http://www.squarespace.com

Payment Sites & Apps

https://www.paypal.com/home

https://squareup.com

Square™ CASH App

Back Up Drives

https://www.dropbox.com

https://www.Google.com/drive/

Stock Images Sites

http://www.Shutterstock.com

http://www.gettyimages.com

http://www.pixabay.com (free images)

http://stock.adobe.com

Glossary: Design Terminology.

Glossary Cited from:

Murdock, Kathy "Graphic Design Terms: Basic Vocabulary You Should Know for Graphic Design" 8April2014

A

Alignment – In graphic design, alignment refers to keeping the elements on the page connected, or aligned, so the elements, when put together, flow well. Each item placed on a page (or web site) should be somehow connected with the others for proper alignment.

B

Bleed – Allowing a graphic or some other element to extend beyond the actual margin of the page. The element touches the side of the page, leaving no margin or white space at the edge.

C

CMYK – This color mode used by printers uses cyan, magenta, yellow and black (CMYK) to create colors during the printing process.

Color Theory – The study of how colors make people feel and their effects on a person. In graphic design, color theory is used to explore the best types of colors to work in different situations: i.e.: for a website that needs to feel soft and relaxing or a magazine ad that should pop out of the page and evoke energy in the reader.

Complementary colors – The colors that are opposite of each other when viewed on the color wheel.

D

DPI – DPI, or dots per inch, refers to

F

Focal point – In graphic design terms, the focal point is where you want to draw the reader's or viewer's eye. This may be large or it may be small. Sometimes graphic designers create a focal point by placing only one tiny object on a page, and in this case the focal point is obvious. Other times the focal point may be within a variety of elements.

G

Grid – An important concept in graphic design, grids are often used in layouts for both web and print projects. Grids help graphic designers arrange text and images on the page in a way that will look even, attractive and consistent throughout. Grids can be used on paper or can be set up in graphic design software, such as Photoshop.

I

Illustrator (Adobe) – Program used by many graphic designers for creating vector images, such as logos and other graphics used for print and online purposes. Those starting out in the program will want to take Adobe Illustrator CS6, which goes over the fundamentals of utilizing Illustrator for graphic design projects.

InDesign (Adobe) – Program used by many graphic designers who deal with magazine, brochure or other print material layouts. Allows the designer or other professional to create a layout, insert photographs or images, add text and send to printer as a completed booklet, pamphlet or other printed item.

K

Kerning – In typography, creating the perfect space between characters (letters) so they work together. For instance, understanding when a letter should be moved slightly because it pushes into another.

L

Line – One of the main elements in graphic design, a line is a mark created using a pen or other tool. Lines form shapes, another element of design. They may be straight, as we often think of them, but they might also be curvy or zig zag.

M

Mock-up – The original design or idea created and either displayed on the screen (for instance, if you are a graphic designer specializing in web design and you want to show your client your ideas before you begin to code you might create a mock-up in Photoshop and then show the client the mock-up as a .jpg or PDF) or in a printed format (for example, a printed copy of the layout for a magazine or brochure spread

for printer's and clients to view before the actual product is produced). Mockups allow the client to see what the final product should look like.

N

Negative space – The area on a page that is left without images and words is referred to as negative or white space. This negative or white space is very important in graphic design projects.

P

Photoshop – Program used by many graphic designers and photographers to create or edit photographs and images. If you are interested in learning more about Photoshop, our Foundations of Photoshop course will get you started with the program.

PPI – PPI, or pixels per inch, refers to the number of pixels per inch in an image.

R

Raster images – These images

are created using thousands of pixels. They are not easily resized as are Vector images; enlarging a raster image too much will diminish quality. Photographs are an example of a raster image.

Resolution – Number of dots per inch, or dpi, in an image. Images for the web are usually be around 72 dpi, or a low resolution, while images for print should be around 300 dpi, or a higher resolution.

RGB – This color mode is used for web design, digital cameras, scanners and other electronics and combines the colors red, green and blue to create what is seen on the screen.

S

Six Elements of Design – Six basic elements are used to create an attractive graphic design project. These include line, shape, value, space, texture and color. Learn more about these six elements in our Introduction to Graphic Design course.

T

Typography – The art of arranging type, which includes letters, numbers and symbols, so that it is pleasing to the eye. This includes not only the font that is used but how it is arranged on the page: letter by letter, size, line spacing, etc. Typography is an important part of creating a pleasing final graphic design product.

Texture – A graphic design term that refers to creating depth to a graphic design product so they have dimension rather than appearing flat. This can be done through the use of patterns behind color, for instance. Learn to add texture to your projects in this class.

V

Vector image – A vector image, such as a logo, is one that can be easily resized without loss of quality.

Author Biography

Timia Williams is a Philadelphia resident born and raised in the City of Brotherly love. She received her Bachelors of Science degree in Graphic Design from The Art Institute of Philadelphia. Her Masters of Science degree in Interactive Media and Design is from Philadelphia University. Ms. Williams has an educational background in Architecture, Fine Art and Graphic Design/Web Design. In 2015, She became a self published author. Her books, including 'Rai Turner's Autobiography of An Adult Entertain' are all available in the on Amazon and Barnesandnoble sites

www.TimiaWilliams.com

Follow her: www.twitter.com/tjwtheauthor
Instagram her: @timiawilliamsgraphics
Email her: tjw183@gmail.com
Facebook: @TimiaJWilliamsDesignandBranding